SNAKES SET II

WATER MOCCASINS

Adam G. Klein
ABDO Publishing Company

visit us at
www.abdopub.com

Published by ABDO Publishing Company, 4940 Viking Drive, Edina, Minnesota 55435.
Copyright © 2006 by Abdo Consulting Group, Inc. International copyrights reserved in all
countries. No part of this book may be reproduced in any form without written permission from
the publisher. The Checkerboard Library™ is a trademark and logo of ABDO Publishing
Company.

Printed in the United States.

Cover Photo: Corbis
Interior Photos: Animals Animals pp. 8, 11, 15, 17, 20; Corbis pp. 7, 19, 21; Getty Images p. 5;
    Peter Arnold p. 9

Series Coordinator: Megan Murphy
Editors: Heidi M. Dahmes, Megan Murphy
Art Direction & Maps: Neil Klinepier

Library of Congress Cataloging-in-Publication Data

Klein, Adam G., 1976-
    Water moccasins / Adam G. Klein.
        p. cm. -- (Snakes. Set II)
    ISBN 1-59679-283-3
    1. Agkistrodon piscivorus--Juvenile literature. I. Title.

QL666.O69K56 2005
597.96'36--dc22

2005048078

CONTENTS

WATER MOCCASINS

Pit vipers belong to the Viperidae **family** of snakes. They make up the subfamily Crotalinae. Pit vipers got their name from the heat-sensing pit on each side of their head. One of the most well-known pit vipers is the water moccasin.

The water moccasin is the only poisonous North American water snake. Its species name is *Agkistrodon piscivorus*. It is also known as the cottonmouth. When this snake feels threatened, it opens its mouth to reveal a cottony white interior.

There are three subspecies of water moccasins. They are the eastern cottonmouth, the western cottonmouth, and the Florida cottonmouth. The differences between each subspecies are slight, and usually based on color.

All snakes are vertebrates, just like humans. This means they have a backbone. They also have scales for skin. Snakes shed their skin several times a year.

Water moccasins enjoy swimming as much as they enjoy basking in the sun!

Sizes

Like most pit vipers, the water moccasin has a stout, heavy body. And it has a distinct, triangle-shaped head. The average length of an adult water moccasin is between 30 and 45 inches (75 and 115 cm). The largest ones can reach 72 inches (183 cm).

People sometimes confuse nonpoisonous snakes with water moccasins. The northern water snake and the Lake Erie water snake look very similar. These harmless snakes are often killed because people think they are water moccasins.

The water moccasin can be **distinguished** by its eye position. Like all pit vipers, this snake has **vertical** pupils. However, its eyes are on the sides of its head. They are protected by a thick ridge of scales. Other water snakes have eyes that are visible from above.

In addition to the thick ridge above their eyes, water moccasins have a broad, dark stripe behind each eye for camouflage.

Colors

Adult water moccasins are dark-colored snakes. They can be olive or brown with wide, black bands that cross their bodies. Older individuals often lose this pattern completely and are mostly black. The water moccasin's belly is usually yellow, and the end of the tail is black.

Young water moccasins are brightly colored with reddish brown crossbands. The colors will become duller and darker as the snake ages. Young water moccasins also have a yellowish tail that they use to attract prey into striking range.

This Florida cottonmouth is preparing to shed. The snake's color looks duller as the old skin separates from the new layer underneath. Once the shed is complete, the color will be brighter.

The water moccasin's color pattern keeps it hidden in the brush and water.

WHERE THEY LIVE

The water moccasin spends most of its time close to or in the water. It is mainly found near swamps, shallow lakes, and slow-moving rivers. It can occasionally be found far from water in trees and bushes, too.

Snakes are cold-blooded creatures. This means they must get their energy from an outside heat source. The water moccasin often spends time in the water. So, it can become cold.

After being in the water, water moccasins **bask** in the sun to recover their body temperature. They find a warm spot in the open to absorb the sun's heat. This is usually on a rock, log, or tree branch at the water's edge. Water moccasins spend much of their day basking.

Water moccasins typically enter the water when they are hunting. The rest of the day they spend basking, hiding, or lying in trees near the water.

WHERE THEY ARE FOUND

The water moccasin is native to the southeastern part of North America. It is found in Virginia, Texas, Oklahoma, Georgia, Florida, and Missouri. There is also a small population in southern Illinois.

Summers in the southeastern United States can be quite hot. Water moccasins like to **bask** in the warm sun. But, they have to be careful not to overheat.

Water moccasins prefer to be most active during the cooler part of the day. So in the summer, they usually hunt at night. They like to hunt in rice fields and **irrigation** ditches. In the spring and fall when it is cooler, they are mainly **diurnal**.

Water moccasins can tolerate cold better than other snakes. So, they start to **hibernate** later than most species. Water moccasins **hibernate** in rock caves, tree stumps, and root holes. They are known to share their dens with rattlesnakes and copperheads.

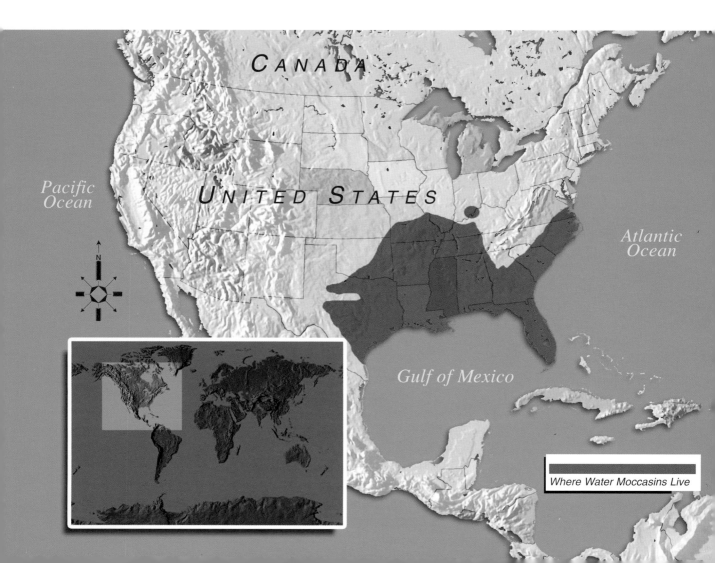

Where Water Moccasins Live

SENSES

Most snakes cannot see very well. They also don't have ears, so they don't hear like humans do. But snakes have other senses that help them survive.

Snakes sense sound through vibrations. As they move along the ground, water moccasins pick up vibrations through bones in their lower jaw.

Like all pit vipers, the water moccasin has a heat-sensing pit on each side of its head. These sensors detect **infrared radiation**, which all living creatures give off. This can lead a snake to its next meal or help the snake avoid **predators**.

Snakes also have a great sense of smell. The water moccasin picks up scent particles with its tongue. On the roof of the snake's mouth is a special sensor called the Jacobson's organ. It allows the snake to determine information about its surroundings.

Water moccasins use their heat-sensing pits to sense creatures from very far away. These sensors are so sharp, they can even detect prey at night!

DEFENSE

The adult water moccasin's main **predators** are alligators and humans. King snakes and large blue snakes are also its natural enemies. Fish, birds, and mammals prey on young water moccasins.

Water moccasins are known to be very **aggressive**. Unlike many snakes, they do not run from danger. The water moccasin will often face its enemies head-on.

When a water moccasin feels threatened, it coils its body and vigorously shakes its tail. At the same time, the water moccasin opens its mouth and gapes at its attacker. This exposes the cottony white interior. If the snake is unable to escape, it will strike, often repeatedly.

The water moccasin is a poisonous snake. It is very dangerous to be bitten by one. Human deaths from its bites are rare, but its **hemotoxic venom** can still cause serious damage. A water moccasin can even bite underwater.

Because of their commonness, large size, and aggressive behavior, water moccasins are among the most dangerous of North America's snakes.

FOOD

The water moccasin's Latin name, *Agkistrodon piscivorus*, means "fish eater." But, water moccasins eat more than just fish. They also eat lizards, frogs, and small mammals. They even eat baby alligators and other snakes!

Water moccasins use their heat-sensing pits to locate their next meal. When hunting in the water, these snakes usually swim with their head above water. After they identify their target, they quickly swim toward it. Then, the water moccasin strikes.

The water moccasin has very powerful jaws. They allow the snake to latch onto its prey. This is different from the quick strike-and-release method of other pit vipers, such as the copperhead.

The water moccasin **injects venom** into its victim through hollow fangs. The victim is held until the venom completely **immobilizes** it. Then, the water moccasin swallows its food headfirst.

Most water moccasins swim with their head above water when they are hunting prey. However, some have been observed exploring with their head beneath the surface.

BABIES

Most female water moccasins have babies every two years. Mating occurs in the spring or fall. Babies are usually born late in the summer.

Mothers do not lay their fertilized eggs like some snake species. Instead, the eggs develop inside of the mother. After three to four months, she is ready to give birth.

A female water moccasin's brood can contain 1 to 15 baby snakes. At birth, the new babies are between 7 and 13 inches (18 and 33 cm) long. And, their **venom** glands are fully developed. This will help the newborn snakes defend themselves and reach **maturity**. Water moccasins can live up to 21 years.

The yellow tail of this young cottonmouth is often used to lure frogs and other small prey.

Young water moccasins are often confused with copperheads because of their similar appearances.

GLOSSARY

aggressive (uh-GREH-sihv) - displaying hostility.

bask - to lie in the heat of the sun.

distinguish - to recognize or indicate as different.

diurnal - active during the day.

family - a group that scientists use to classify similar plants or animals. It ranks above a genus and below an order.

hemotoxic - harmful to the circulatory system of the body.

hibernate - to spend the winter in an inactive state.

immobilize - to make someone or something unable to move or be moved.

infrared radiation - energy that is given off as waves of heat.

inject - to forcefully introduce a fluid into the body, usually with a needle or something sharp.

irrigation - supplying land with water by using channels, streams, and pipes.

maturity - the state of having reached full growth or development.

predator - an animal that kills and eats other animals.

venom - a poison produced by some animals and insects. It usually enters a victim through a bite or sting.

vertical - in the up-and-down position.

WEB SITES

To learn more about water moccasins, visit ABDO Publishing Company on the World Wide Web at **www.abdopub.com**. Web sites about these snakes are featured on our Book Links page. These links are routinely monitored and updated to provide the most current information available.

INDEX